I0828196

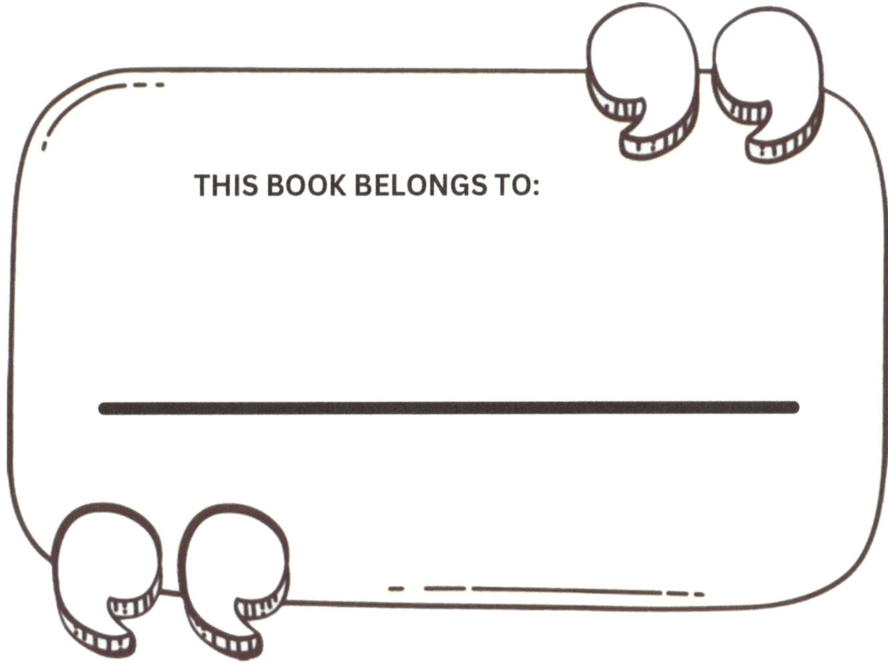
THIS BOOK BELONGS TO:

WELCOME
TO
MONTANA

MONTANA
ORO Y PLATA

Dedicated to all the explorers.

ISBN 978-1-958985-93-9

www.joeysavestheday.com

Mimi Books™ Publishing

A Mimi Book

Montana got its name from the Spanish word "montaña," which means "mountain." Early settlers chose the name because of the state's tall peaks and rugged landscapes. Over time, the name "Montana" became the perfect fit for the wide-open spaces and beautiful mountain ranges the state is known for today.

Montana's history begins with Native American nations such as the Crow, Blackfeet, Salish, and Kootenai, who lived on the plains and in the mountains for thousands of years. In the 1800s, explorers and fur traders arrived, followed by gold miners hoping to strike it rich. As towns grew, Montana became part of the United States. Today, Montana is known for its wide-open prairies, tall mountains, and a history shaped by the people who have called it home.

Montana was the forty-first state to join the Union. It officially joined on November 8, 1889.

41st

Montana is located in the northwestern United States. It is bordered by Idaho, Wyoming, North Dakota, and South Dakota. To the north, it meets the Canadian provinces of British Columbia, Alberta, and Saskatchewan.

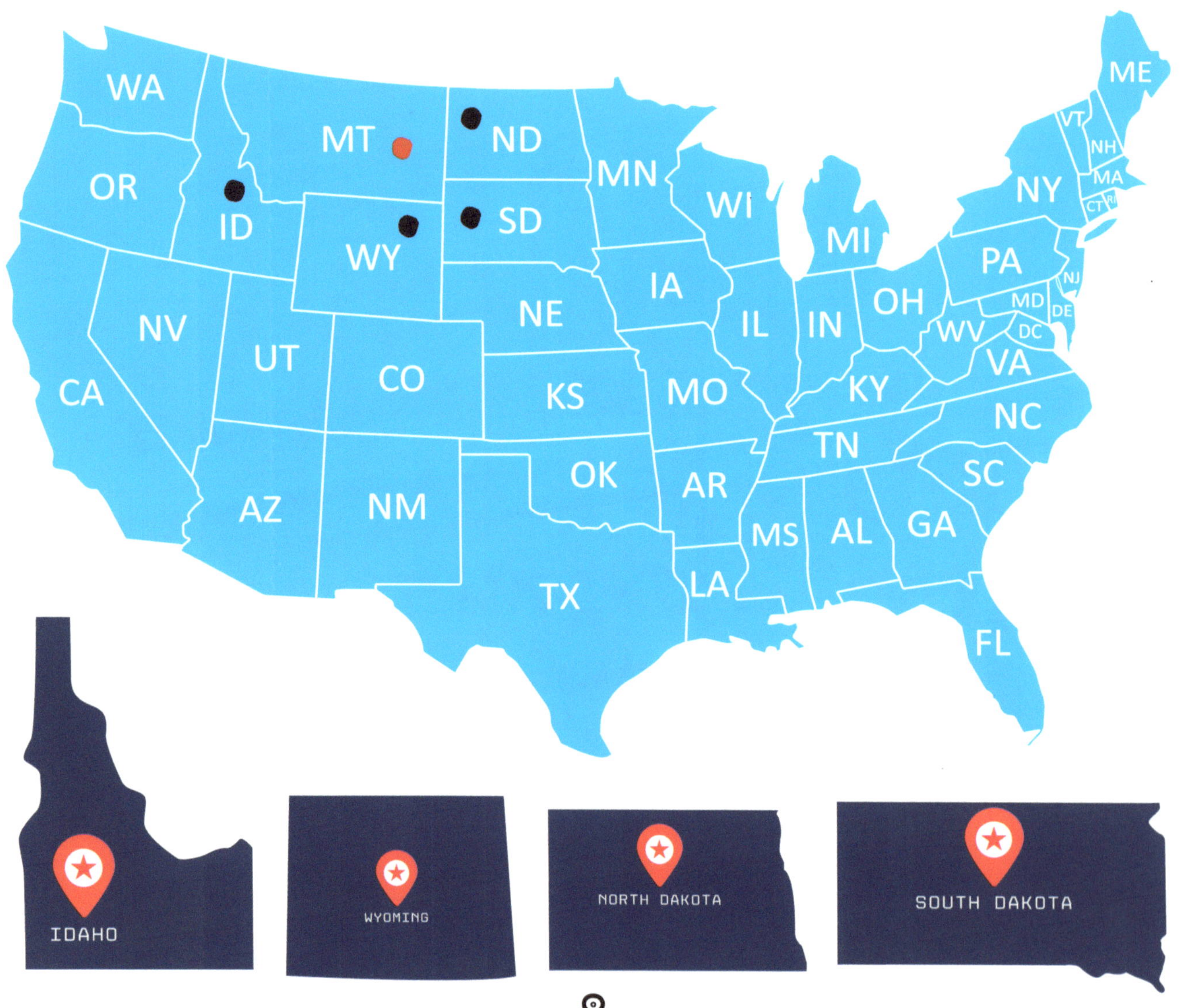

Helena is the capital of Montana.
It officially became the capital in 1894.

Billings, Montana, has an estimated population of about 119,400 people.

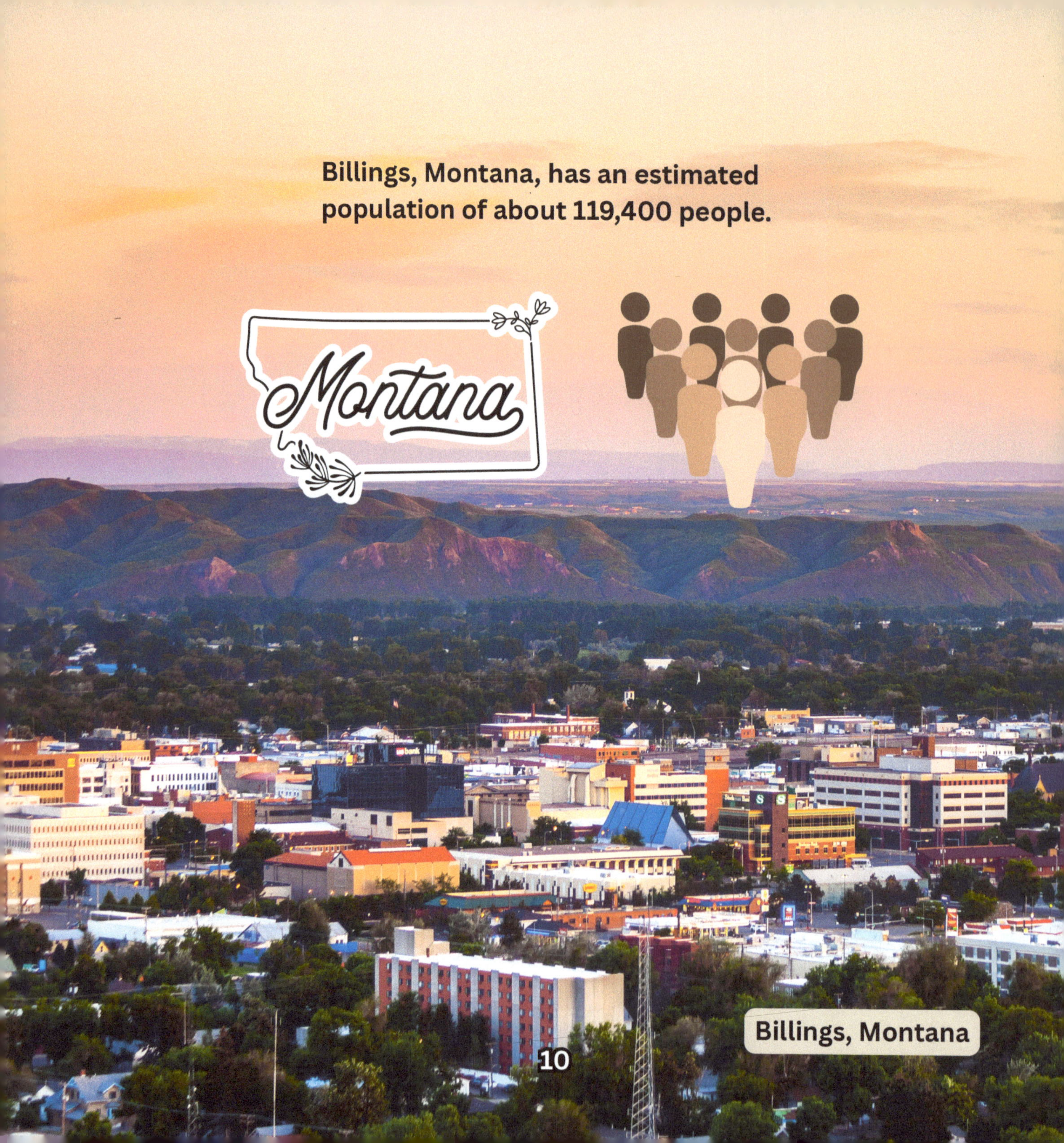

Billings, Montana

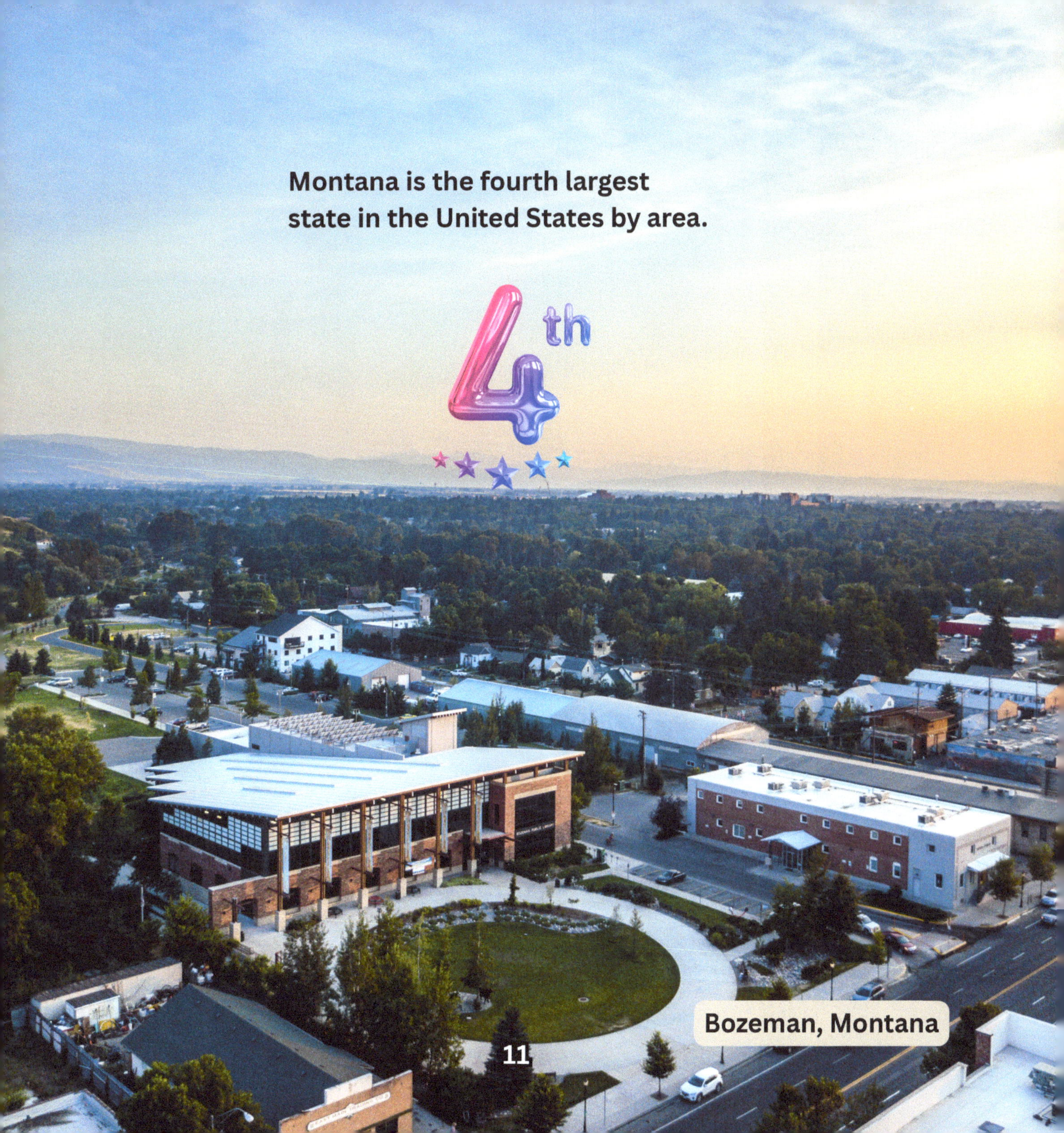
Montana is the fourth largest state in the United States by area.
4th
Bozeman, Montana

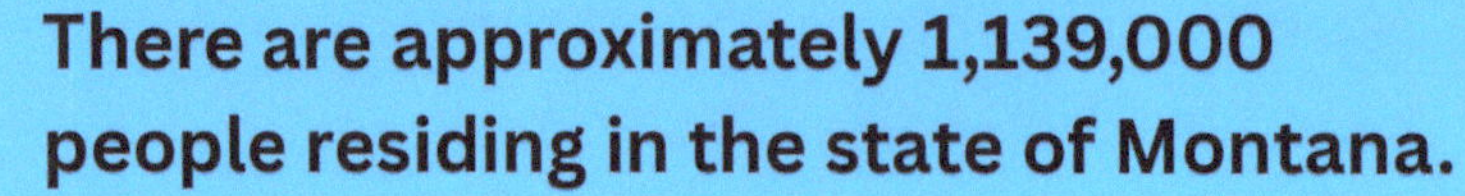

There are approximately 1,139,000 people residing in the state of Montana.

Missoula, Montana

Charles M. Russell was born on March 19, 1864, in St. Louis, Missouri, but he spent most of his life in Montana, which is where he found his inspiration. He lived in places like Utica and later Great Falls, where he created hundreds of paintings and sculptures that showed cowboys, horses, and Native American life in the Old West. Russell loved Montana's wide-open spaces, and his artwork helps people imagine what life looked like long ago. Today, he is remembered as one of Montana's most important and beloved artists.

Montana is known for its tasty pasties (pronounced PASS-tees), warm, handheld pies filled with meat, potatoes, and vegetables. Miners brought this cozy meal to Montana long ago because it was easy to carry and stayed warm for a long time. Families across the state still enjoy pasties today, especially on chilly days, making them one of Montana's most comforting and traditional foods.

Enjoy

MONTANA

There are 56 counties in Montana.

Here is a list of twenty of those counties:

Carbon	Fallon	Granite	Powell
Carter	Fergus	Hill	Prairie
Cascade	Flathead	Jefferson	Ravalli
Chouteau	Gallatin	Judith Basin	Richland
Custer	Garfield	Lake	Roosevelt

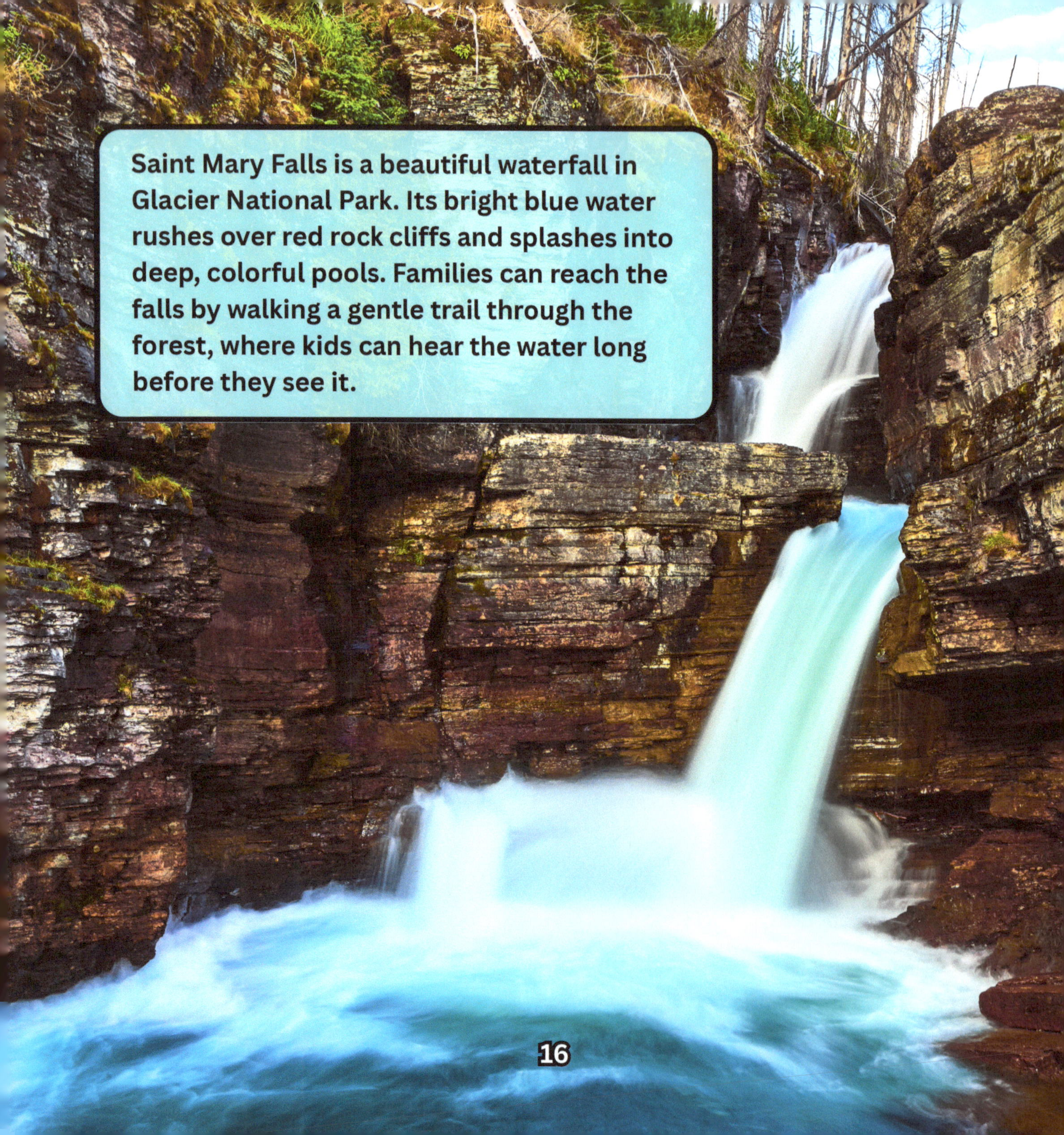

Saint Mary Falls is a beautiful waterfall in Glacier National Park. Its bright blue water rushes over red rock cliffs and splashes into deep, colorful pools. Families can reach the falls by walking a gentle trail through the forest, where kids can hear the water long before they see it.

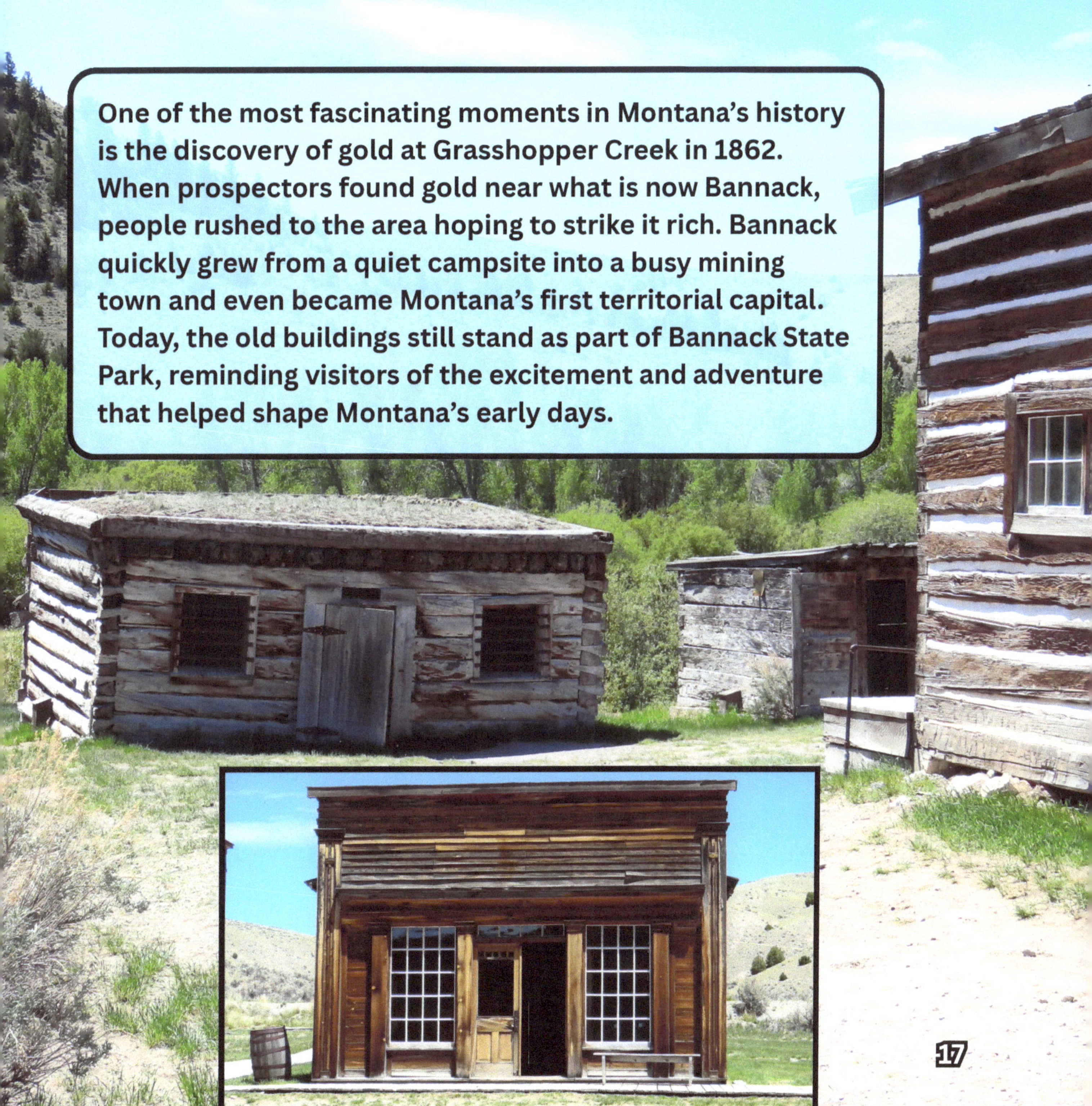

One of the most fascinating moments in Montana's history is the discovery of gold at Grasshopper Creek in 1862. When prospectors found gold near what is now Bannack, people rushed to the area hoping to strike it rich. Bannack quickly grew from a quiet campsite into a busy mining town and even became Montana's first territorial capital. Today, the old buildings still stand as part of Bannack State Park, reminding visitors of the excitement and adventure that helped shape Montana's early days.

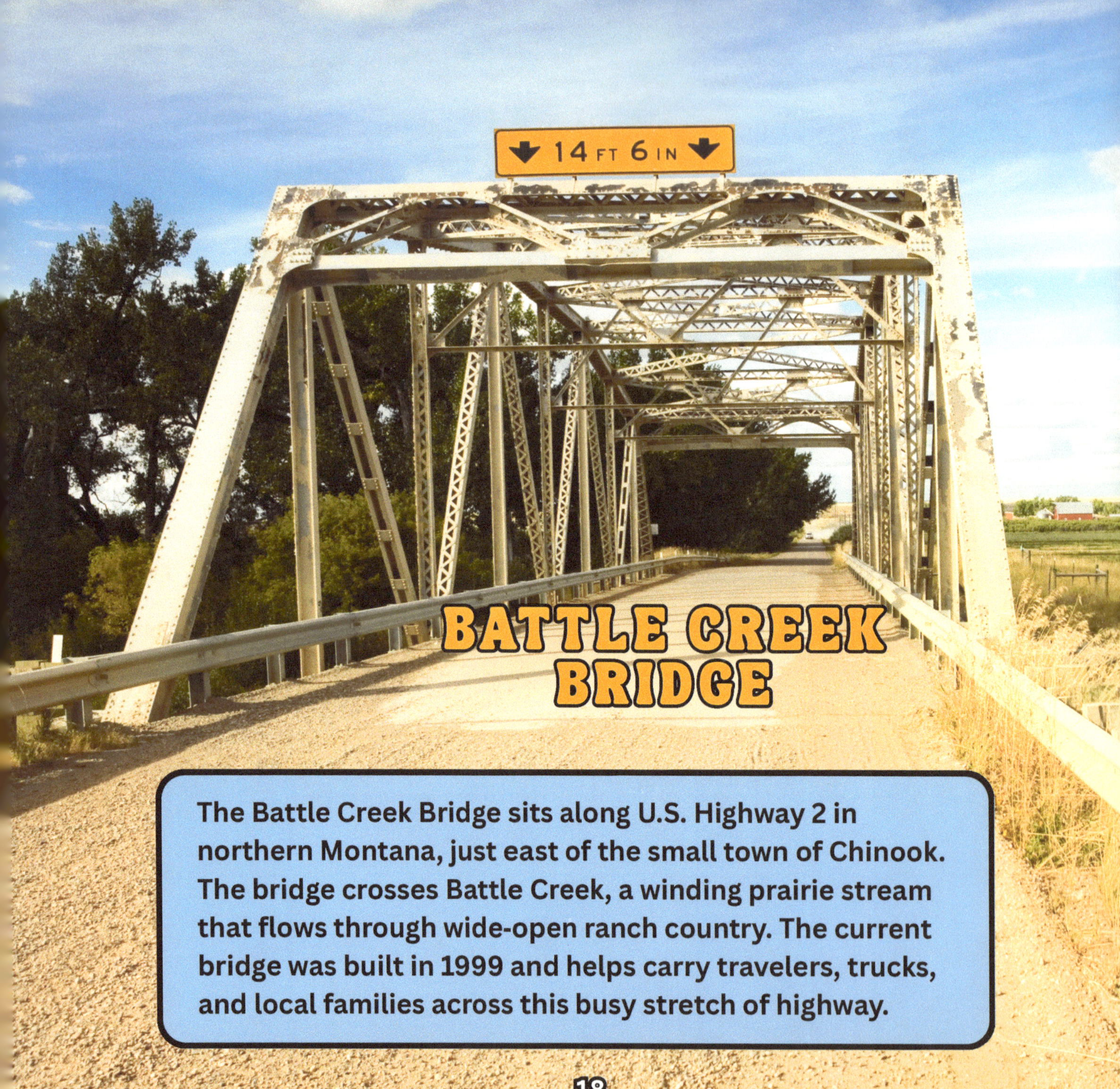

BATTLE CREEK BRIDGE

The Battle Creek Bridge sits along U.S. Highway 2 in northern Montana, just east of the small town of Chinook. The bridge crosses Battle Creek, a winding prairie stream that flows through wide-open ranch country. The current bridge was built in 1999 and helps carry travelers, trucks, and local families across this busy stretch of highway.

The Montana state bird is the Western Meadowlark. It became the official state bird in 1931.

The official state flower of Montana is the Bitterroot. It was chosen as the state flower in 1895.

A couple of Montana's nicknames include Big Sky Country and the Treasure State.

ST8

Montana's state motto is "Oro y Plata," which means "Gold and Silver." It was adopted in 1865.

The abbreviation for Montana is MT.

MT

Montana's state flag was officially adopted in 1905.

Some crops grown in Montana are wheat, barley, sugar beets, and hay.

Some animals that live in Montana are elk, grizzly bears, gray wolves, mountain lions, and bald eagles.

Montana experiences a wide range of temperatures throughout the year. The hottest temperature ever recorded in the state was 117 degrees Fahrenheit, measured in Glendive on July 20, 1893. In contrast, the coldest temperature documented was –70 degrees Fahrenheit, recorded at Rogers Pass on January 20, 1954.

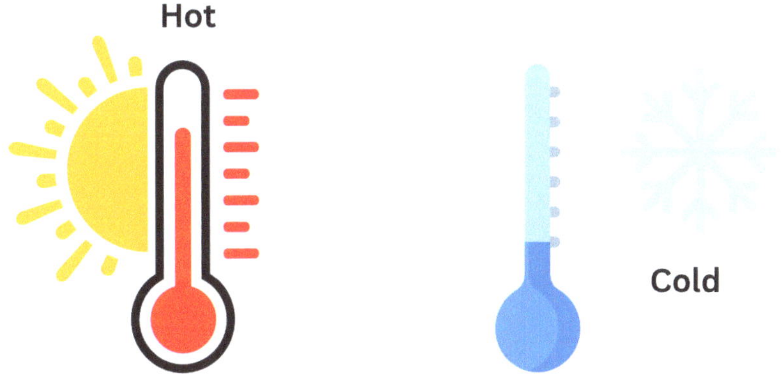

ZooMontana in Billings is a wonderful place to explore, with animals from many different habitats. Kids can see grizzly bears, wolves, bison, otters, and playful monkeys, along with colorful birds and reptiles.

The Battle of the Little Bighorn took place in 1876 in what is now Montana. It was an important moment in history where Lakota, Cheyenne, and Arapaho warriors defended their land. Today, the Little Bighorn Battlefield is a national monument where people can learn about Native American history and the events that shaped the West.

The largest airport in Montana is Bozeman Yellowstone International Airport, located in Belgrade, near Bozeman. It sits at 850 Gallatin Field Road and serves as the main travel hub for people flying in and out of Montana. This airport connects travelers to cities across the country and provides easy access to Montana's mountains, parks, and outdoor adventures, including Yellowstone National Park.

The Missoula PaddleHeads are a Minor League Baseball team based in Missoula, a lively city in western Montana. They play their home games at Ogren Park at Allegiance Field, a bright and cheerful ballpark known for its fun family atmosphere and beautiful mountain views. The PaddleHeads are part of the Pioneer League, and many young players spend time on this team as they build their skills and work toward their baseball dreams.

FOOTBALL

The Montana Grizzlies are one of the most popular football teams in the state, and families all across Montana cheer for them every season. The team plays its home games at Washington–Grizzly Stadium in Missoula, a loud and energetic stadium surrounded by beautiful mountain views. Fans wearing maroon and silver pack the stands, creating one of the most exciting game-day atmospheres in college football.

The ponderosa pine is Montana's state tree. It's known for its tall, sturdy trunk and long needles that give forests a fresh, piney smell. The ponderosa pine was officially adopted as the state tree in 1949, and its towering height and warm, orange-brown bark have made it a proud symbol of Montana's wide forests and natural beauty.

The blackspotted cutthroat trout is Montana's state fish. It's a colorful trout known for the small black spots along its body and the bright red streaks under its jaw. This beautiful fish lives in clear, cold rivers and mountain streams across the state. It was officially adopted as Montana's state fish in 1977.

Can you name these?

I hope you enjoyed learning about Montana.

To explore fun facts about the other 49 states, visit my website at www.joeysavestheday.com. You'll also find a wide variety of homeschool resources to support joyful learning at home. If you enjoyed this book, I would be grateful if you left a review. Your feedback truly helps. Thank you for your support!

Check out these other interesting books in the 50 States Fact Books Series!

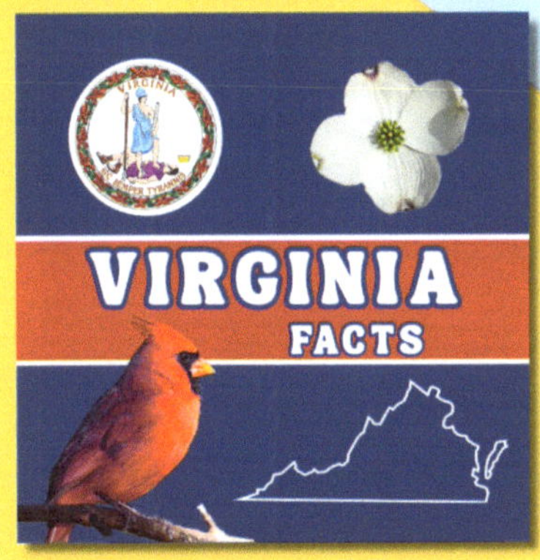

www.ingramcontent.com/pod-product-compliance
Lightning Source LLC
LaVergne TN
LVHW070200110826
845147LV00002B/458

9781958985939